Like Dorothy

Memoirs of a Teen

Claudia Villa Mora

authorHOUSE®

AuthorHouse™ UK Ltd.
500 Avebury Boulevard
Central Milton Keynes, MK9 2BE
www.authorhouse.co.uk
Phone: 08001974150

First published by AuthorHouse 1/26/2009

ISBN: 978-1-4389-0287-6 (sc)

Printed in the United States of America
Bloomington, Indiana

This book is printed on acid-free paper.

To my brothers:
Octavio, Manny, Beto, and Rodrigo.

And to Martine Benatar for simply listening.

This book is based upon some real life events of the author. Dramatical changes have been made for further protection and privacy.

"If you read,
        You'll judge"
                -Kurt Cobain

Acknowledgements

This book was written for those who have experienced the painful lost and confusion of losing a significant other in their life. It is also written in loving memory of every suicide victim. The national suicide rate victims is; 11 suicides per every 100,000 people.

Keep in mind that:

According to the National Institute of Mental Health, depression affects 17 million Americans a year.

One out of four women will eventually suffer from severe or mild depression in their lifetime.
For men, it is one in eight.

Amber

At birth I was given the name of Amber.
Father had chosen it to be that way,
for he adored the grain fields of amber back on
Grandfather's ranch.

The evening I was born, tons of golden fall leaves piled up so that
he could see them through Mother's room while she
screamed and pushed for me to be born.

The Perfect Four

Right after labor,
It had been just Mother and I struggling in the big city of LA
all by ourselves.

Until Father's conscience bit him
and he decided to join us in our journey.

We then flew over to Grandfather's ranch in Alabama
where Mother often whined about Father
and Father often yelled to Mother.

So in its due time it became only
Mona (a small doll Grandpa had given me), Grandma,
Grandpa himself, and I. The perfect family of four.

My Family

I can recollect the memories used up
in that wooden bench outside that faced our fields.

The four of us would huddle around that huge woven blanket.
And count the stars at twilight, tied up as one.

The Gift

Mother had always said I was born gifted
 with the powers of astrology.

At nights I had these abnormal dreams,
which most of the time came true to me.

Once I had a dream with an image of a baby.
Days later Auntie Emma announced her pregnancy.

Creepy? I know.

I had a dream with death once.
I became frightened to sleep at night.

A week later Grandfather lay in a funeral box.

I hated my gift!

Remembering the Dead

There lay the carcass
deep inside that blue, wooden box.

Holding Grandpa's weak, stiffening body
asleep.

I know he's asleep.
I can hear him breathe.
I can hear his soul knocking,
begging to be free.

I caress his hair,
hold his cold, clammy skin.

I breathe death through my pores
and awake only to find
corpses surrounding my bed.

We Would

We would
Crawl underneath Grandpa's couch.

We would
Over pour blossom scents of lotion on his feet.

We would
Massage his tense muscles and giggle
once we heard him snore.

We would
Kiss his cheek goodbye.

Grandma would hand us a token of gratitude, and
we would come back another night.

How we miss him now
that he's gone.

Dead Crops

The ripest tomato has fallen
into a field that no one looks out for any more,
that no one dares to touch.

The crops have vanished
 with your ashes,
 with my soul,
to a land of the unknown!

New Skin

The girl that was once easily amused,
that solitary child that baked with Grandma,
and was in charge of dressing Mona every morning,
was now living in the city,
where the clouds feed off the smog,
and had converted into a sociable young lady
with a curvier frame,
sensitive breast,
and was now in charge of checking her calendar every month.

The Night Before Dad Left Us

Seeing Daddy like this harms me.
Of course we haven't gotten along lately,
ever since my breasts grew and I started liking boys.

He says he wants to leave.
He says he's no longer happy here.

Marriage has been a hard thing on him.
Each day, I watch as wide lines stretch out on his forehead.

So there he is thinking,
out in the dark, sipping on a beer.

While Mother sleeps.

I think he might leave now.
I think he might leave us forever.
And I can't imagine what forever will be like.

I used to be Daddy's girl,
back before my breasts grew
and I started liking boys.

I'd follow him everywhere he'd go.
He was the most precious man to me
aside from Grandpa.

First Crush

When I was five
I skipped in the playground with my tiny tennis shoes,
the ones that lit up once you jumped in 'em.

When I was five
I wept when Mommy drove me down to school.

I never dared to hold a boy's hand;
they all had "cooties"—you know, germs!

Once, a boy gathered some fresh-cut flowers for me.
Huge, golden sunflowers and dandelions.

The dandelions I instantly blew on his face...
with a smirk.

The sunflowers I kept...
though they died by the time I realized they were
meant to be kept in fresh water.

But, I cherished them so.
You were my first crush.
I then realized it with a blush.

Cyber-Love

My stomach is like a net,
catching butterflies.

When the clock reads nine o' clock and I meet
with you on cyber space.

When I read your voice online,
when I reach out for the keyboard to respond to you,
I can forget all about Grandpa's death and my parents filing for divorce.
It's like you have the power to save my heart from all that makes it sink.

Hopes

I hope
he's not a joke.

I hope
he doesn't smoke.

I hope
he's real.

I hope
he loves me so.

The Meeting

I rushed to the bathroom,
applied Mom's expensive makeup,
fixed my hair the best I could.

When I heard you were coming over to meet me,
I was anxious to meet the guy who had been making my heart dance online.

How It Occurred

After our first date we arranged to meet for the second time at a local party.
That same weekend my parents had gone to visit Grandmother without me.

 It was getting quite late
and there was still no sign of him.

After I had chugged just about a jillion mixed vodka drinks,
I spotted him from far away. There he stood looking
for me in between the wild crowd of teens.

He had a worried look in those crystal clear eyes of his
that nearly drove me crazy.

For a second I thought of running and avoiding such embarrassment.

But, what really happened was that I had lost sight of him, and before I was
even able to take a step further, I felt a hand tapping my shoulder, and he said,
" Hi. I'm looking for a beautiful girl named Amber."

And I blushed and smiled,
without saying a single word.

He then leaned forward and kissed me.
Suddenly my knees grew weak,
and I'm pretty sure I kissed him back.

He

He has the silkiest strands of blonde hair I've ever seen,
like those models who pose for *Pantene Pro-V* products.

He has thin lips,
which I decisively adore biting.

He has long arms
whose occupation are to hold me.

He owns a guitar
that plays tunes to my soul.

But, above all,
he has my heart.

Spaced-Out during Chemistry Class

When Ms. Barley
questions me in reference
to protons and electrons,
all I can focus on is the
directions our bodies took
when they bonded for that very first time.

And just when Ms. Barley is expecting my answer,
and the whole class starts giggling,

the bell rings, and I'm literally saved by the bell!

Between Passing Periods

I make my way through the hall and spot
my best friend, Judy,
along with her boyfriend,
making out
underneath the stairway.

And I whisper to her, "You're gonna be late."

Oh, and I just can't wait
for it to be after school.

After School

I'm sitting alone
on the bench
as the others leap onto the yellow bus.

Anxiously, I wait for you.

And when I hear the honking of your
automobile, I jump out of joy,
cheering for this afternoon to never end.

At His House

I meet his mother, who happens to be very kind
and comes to believe I am very decent for her son.

Then I leave the room with him
as he searches for a spot behind his door
where our lips brush off and our tongues practically
reach.

And suddenly I feel like I've been filmed for one of those
sex tapes,

and I come to judge myself,
as if I'm still aware that lady just mentioned I was decent.

From Heaven to Hell

Everything happened so quickly;
it was as if from one day to another
my passion for him had awakened.

I had mastered hiding all my tragic emotions
when I was near him, in fear of ruining the moments spent.

Everything was wonderful by his side;
the hours spent were like seconds for me.

And when I would return home,
I realized I returned alone.

Because I could no longer tolerate
the silence as I stepped in our door.

I had been from heaven to hell
in a small matter of time.

He was my joy.

And my misery was
Mother's sorrowful appearance,
along with the smell of the ten cigarettes she had inhaled for the day.

Little Signs

You would hold my hand in public.
You would protect me from all evil.
You would listen to me.
You would play fight with me,
making sure I never lost my smile.

Now you walked ahead of me in public.
Didn't bother if people tormented me.
Now you would skip our phone calls.
Now play fighting wasn't our thing.

Dirty Reflection

Right beneath those brown eyes,
I could see my reflection.
Inside you're angry; you're hurt just like me.

When you gave out your heart, they tore you apart.

Look into my eyes, and say that you don't think I'm stunning.
Because what we are is all we've got.

Addict

There's an addict
with ruby heels,
short tank top,
and bleached jeans
sitting on the porch.

There's an addict
waiting out for her drug to re-appear.

Smoking pot,
flipping channels through the big screen,
listening to rock.

Having sex
as the drug feeds the addict.

The New You

That became the new you.
You became my maddest addiction.

In You

You seized losing me in your insides,
bewitching me with each stare.
Your spirit tangled in mine.
Hushing me with your net,
toxiferous touch.
Feeding me with your pecks,
I sinned in you. In your tissues,
precious weaves,
I converted in you,
sadly in you!

I Said:

If you don't want children,
It's all right—we won't have them.

I will have my own.
I will raise 'em
and feed 'em
and tell 'em,
"Daddy loves you so."

You said:
you loved me, so
then you must've meant it, right?

You said:
you would love our children more than anything.

But you said, we couldn't keep her.
You didn't want to keep her.

I knew you didn't want me by your side.
I knew you didn't want to watch my enormous
belly stretch as I carried our children.

So I didn't want her either.
I didn't want anything of yours.

The Abortion

So we had a kid;
I named it Apple.

You never met her
of course.

I greeted the tiny fetus
as it crawled out of my uterus.
Vibrant stains in the clinic's bed.

We had a daughter.
At least I like to believe we once did.
Her name was Apple…
But you never met her of course.

Metro

I sat soaked in tears,
outside in the metro bus stop.
Outside of the clinic were I aborted Apple.

A hideous lady sat next to me
as she waited for the same bus as I did.

She was hideous outside;
inside she was beautiful.

She had a blonde-reddish, thick mustache
like that of Amish men.
Her face was covered with
scars of acne.
And
her body was like a replica of a sumo wrestler's.

She then sang a prayer for me
"Oh God," she said, "help the youth."

And I said, "Oh God, please don't let me grow as ugly as her."

Now I know beauty isn't all.
Back then I didn't know.

Something in the Air

There's something in the air
that feels so incomplete.

There's something in the air
that makes me want to screech.

There's something in the air,
that silence,
that fear,
that mist of ignorance.

There's something in the air
that has been drawing you away from me.

And I

And I didn't recognize your smell anymore;
your touch was meaningless to me.

And I knew what had been mine
was no longer mine.

And I realized I had discharged all my negativity
against your shoulders.

And I knew I shouldn't have hidden my problems at home
because you too had your own.

And I knew we were both to blame.

And I waited
for your eyes to shut down when they coldly turned my way .

And I ran as far as I could
with no direction as to where I was going.

And I didn't bother to turn back,
even when you called my name...

Ambeeeeeeeeeeer!

That Night

After the argument,
after the break-up,
you wouldn't answer your phone.

Mother was sleeping,
Father was at his new home.

There stood thirty or perhaps more pills,
that lay neatly In my palm before I
washed them down with a tall glass of water.

Never did I fear.
All I wanted was to not feel this lonesome,
the grief of losing someone once more.

Minutes later I must have fainted,
the way typical Hollywood movie stars faint in those dramatic scenes.
I opened my eyes and appeared in what seemed to me as Munchkin land.

Charcoal

Ice tea used to be my favorite drink.
Pink lemonade was a must in summer.

Charcoal mixed in water became a remedy
to eject
the high dose I had absorbed.

An extensive tube entered my mouth
as I made my way unconsciously to the E.R.

I realize now the carbonaceous substance saved my life.
I realize now it wasn't my time to depart this world.

I realized from there on, I belonged in a mental institute.

Room III

There is a pretty girl resting on the other side of the room.
And all I see is a dirty shadow to my left on the window,
which appears to be me.

I Wonder

Grandma Dora said,
that ever since Grandpa Joe died
she started sweating.

I became amused hearing her say
bizarre things like these.

I pictured her
as if she had never sweated
before in her life.

Like if she had never dripped
a single drop of salty sweat
down her forehead before.

And when she did,
I felt as if her sweat were tears
running down her face, and I wondered....

What kind of strange stories Mom would have said
about me, if I had died that September night as I chugged
those capsules down my throat?

As I was to commit a self-crime.
The crime of suicide.

But, instead I lay here wondering.
I lay in this hospital bed.
Not like your ordinary hospital, actually,
for here they're all INSANE!

Grandma Said:

"Grandpa and Auntie Sarah
are in a better place now."

I said,
"Why didn't they take me with 'em?"

The Root

I don't know what exactly caused it—
which was the root that dried up the flower?

Perchance it was the yelling in Dad's voice
when he said I was using Grandpa's death
as an excuse to get out of school earlier
than the other kids.

Or maybe it was the look you gave me
when you said it was over; that scared me.

Reasonably it was the Sunday dress I
wore to mass the day before.
I knew I shouldn't have listened to Mother
when she suggested I wear that pastel
pink dress that made me feel like such
a "girlie girl."

Possibly

Possibly it was you who dragged me
and carried me into the bright red automobile.
The one that cried as loud as my mother did
the day Dad asked her for their divorce.

But who am I to blame?
Who am I to choose my fortune?

Gulp...gulp...swallow...
"Lift up your tongue and let me see it go down your throat,"
said Bertha,
the big-shaped nurse who carried our meds.

Group Talk

Today we were forced to huddle around
the carpet for a group talk.

I glare at the fury in the other patients' eyes.

Our bodies had formed a circle;
as that circle went around we were introduced.

Ryan: ran away from home twice; like a psycho
he was living in the streets of California along with
some heroin addicts who he claims as his only family.
A cop who turned him in found him.

Yvonne: is my age; she was caught drugged in a basement
while having sex with multiple partners.

Molly: is the girl who shares a bedroom with me. She was brought in by
her father after having severe panic attacks.

As my turn comes around,
I shake in fear,
ashamed.

I'm trying to remember why am I here again.

"Hi. My name is Amber, and I'm NUTS!"

Letter to Mom

Dear Mom,

I'm going crazy,
I really am.

My brain is dislocated;
like a puzzle, piece me back.

The clock unwinds and talks to me.
It tells me stories from the past.

I smell my room burning up at night.

Poking wires come and greet me
from outside,
crawling through my window.

You complain as to why didn't
I ask for your help on time.

As if I never looked insane to you before.
As if you never noticed my bad posture.

All you did was sit and cry!

The Wizard

It's like I'm trapped in this building with munchkins.
With nutty, idiotic, loud munchkins.

It's like were all off to see the Wizard to help us find a piece of mind.

I need no Wizard.
I need no piece of mind.
I've got my own.

All I need is my ruby slipper' s and I'm set to go!

The Prozac Lady

There's this lady
hovering through our halls at night,
wearing nothing but white.

She's
knocking in every single room
serving Prozac to you and I.

This lady, I tell you, she says,
"This will drain all your pains.
Like magic it will make 'em go all away!"

Don't miss a single dose!
Come here, let's have a toast!

CHEERS!

Drunken Fornication

Before my parents filed for divorce,
I heard a couple moaning once,
as a little girl.

The man was heavily drunk,
enjoying himself inside his
wife's body.

The wife tried not to make
a single sound, to not wake up
her child, asleep, who lay
right beside her, just footsteps away.

But, she couldn't help it and
breathed heavily in pain or perhaps joy.

The bed cried loudly.

As a little girl, I had trouble sleeping.

Why?

Why can't you come visit me?
Why didn't you grow as erratic as me?
Why must I face this all alone?

Do you not know I'm trapped here?
Should you know?
Do I really want you to know?
...Okay maybe not!

I Want to Know

I wanna know where your yesterdays hide. I can't
imagine what your todays are like.

Without you.
Without me.

I wanna breathe your air for just a minute, to remind me that I'm not alone.

I see you in my most abstract dreams; you're alive!

Remember

Remember the day we got caught in the rain, and how ill you got when you were soaking wet?

We hid under your hut, and I massaged your sleepy head until you fell asleep.

When you were sick I took care of you.
Remember?

Cope

For a year I coped with "rock candy"—
crystal meth, that is.

For days I watched the fire burn
my skin.

For years I was addicted to a
bad relationship,

obsessed with its dominance.
How it fucked with my self-esteem,

until I swallowed those pills,
until I was brought here,

only to swallow some more meds
and perhaps learn how to cope;
all I do is hope!

Mother

From the instant Grandfather passed away,
I grew sick.

I remember not getting a single second of rest
for about three days.

And even then, when I had evolved into a total zombie,
Mother prohibited the use of any tranquilizers.

Now, I can have 'em here!
They encourage me to take them.

They say I must,
or else I'll grow as schizoid as Molly.

They are my drug dealers,
and
I am their guinea pig.

Six a.m. Showers

I like the sensation of the crisp water,
the way it rushes through my skin.

I wonder if it can take me.
with its flow,
with its power.

Watch as the drain sucks me in,
drawing my body towards it.

I like the sensation of the crisp water,
the way it touches my skin,
makes me feel alive.

Mirror, Mirror on the Wall

Sometimes I stare at my image
in the rusty mirror on our wall
for minutes, then hours.

Until my pores turn into nothing.

Until my image seems unclear,
almost unrecognizable.

And then I realize
it's not me who I'm starring at.

And then I realize
it's a waste of my time.

Bare Naked

I indulge sleeping naked
and feeling the silkiness of my skin
rub against the bed sheets.

I admire the softness of my skin.
Its warmth, the way it wraps around me.

When I lay with nothing but
my bare nudity and no one but myself,
I see beauty in what
society views as imperfect.

But, when I lay undressed
in the sheets of this foul mattress,
Bertha thinks it's perverse
and declares me even more insane.

Phone Calls

Phone calls are kept short and
supervised under a clear, glass window.

Conversations are awkward
and filled with complete silence.

I can smell your pity from here,
I get sick from dialing all those numbers.
And when the phone rings
I grow even more insane.

So when it's my turn
and I'm allowed to make phone calls,
I just hang up the phone and
make my way back to my room.

Tina

The fragile image of a girl with anorexia nervosa
makes her entrance into the dining room
but, of course, refuses to eat anything at all.

She's petrified of consuming her bowl of soup
and believes that if she does,
her whole body will bloat as big as a
hippo's.

Come to think of it,

I share that same fear with her.

Falls Leaves

She is like a tiny fall leaf to me.
Like those leaves I view from the outside,
running at such a speed.

Lightweight leaves with
such beautiful colors of fall.

I want to be just like her!

Pale, yellow complexion,
ash-brown streams of hair,
wine lips.

Lightweight like a leaf.
Ninety pounds, I estimate.

She is like a tiny fall leaf to me.

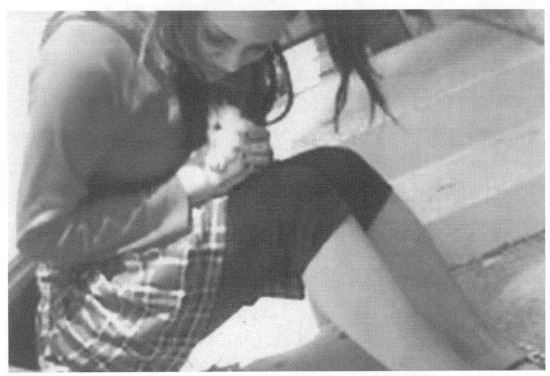

Dad and I at a restaurant in Mexico.

A year later. Mom and I (looking healthier than ever).

During Lunch

There's this huge fly
starring at Molly and I.
It's glued to the glass window
with bug eyes as huge as ours.

Molly is totally grossed out by it.

I'm trying to ignore it.
Either way, I wasn't planning on eating my lunch today.
They feed us so much here that I'm thinking by the time I'm let out
I may grow to be as obese as Bertha, our nurse.

Molly is over annoyed by it now.

She then raises a hardcover book up to the sky,
intent on killing the poor thing.

Instantly the fly that one day flew outside,
mellowed in the carpet floor,
DEAD.

Thoughts about Death

I'm contemplating,
concluding
that everything I love in this life will one day vanish.

Like Dorothy

Like Dorothy,
I tap my imaginary ruby slippers.

And rub 'em against each other,
whispering, "There's no place like home,
there's no place like home....
sweet, sweet, home,"

wishing that when I opened my eyes,
I'd appear in my own Emerald City.

Brain Surgery

Next time you come and visit,
I promise I won't talk to you
about these horrible, green gowns
they make us wear here.

Next time you come and visit,
I'll sharpen my tools
and hand you a sketch
on how to perform a brain surgery
on me.

Then you can open my head,
escort the lunatic cells out of my brain,

like if it were a soaked sponge caught up
in bad rain.

Then you'll hang it outside
on a tree or on a branch,

until it magically
grows new cells,

until it reproduces new liquids.

Once it's safe enough,
place it back in my head,

kiss my forehead,
and let me know everything will be okay again!

During Meals

During meals Tina occasionally sits next to me.

She observes me as I chew my food down,

and for a moment I consider her a spy.

When we are dismissed from meals,
she runs to the nearest restroom,

where she sticks her fingers
down her throat in madness and repugnance

to prevent those extra pounds.

Monkey See, Monkey Do

I had 205 grains of rice today.
Tina observed me the whole time.

I had 205 grains of rice today,
but I threw them all away.

I fed it to the wide-mouthed
toilet seat.

A pool of my own debris.

Molly the Strange

Molly says her boyfriend loves her a lot,
that he worries she's in here.

Her father approves of their relationship.

Her mother forsook her,
once she found out she was ill.

Her parents are divorced;
her boyfriend is all she's got.

And when he visits her
and kisses her, she gets sulky,
unglued maybe.

I think she's strange.
I think I'm sane when I'm around her.

Movie Night

On Friday we had movie night.
We each were to gather our remaining
spare change for pizza and snacks.

The change we would have received from our parents on Sundays,
when they usually came by for visits.

The quarters and dimes we would collect in a clear urine
Container, which was handed out to us by Bertha.
 Whenever we wanted to make
 a phone call we reached out for it.
It's not like there was much to waste it on.

When it was Molly's turn
to pitch in her part for the pizza party,
she took out a urine cup that
overflowed with folded dollar bills.

When I asked her who had given it to her,
she looked at me in shock and pointed outside.
Then she locked in fear,
like a wild deer would out in the woods,
 about to be attacked by a predator.

She had sworn she'd seen a man
from the outside window staring at her.
I told her there was nothing out there,
and her fear grew even more.

She kicked and screamed,
trying to defend herself from that man.
Of course there was nothing, no such thing as
a man who was trying to fight her.

She was from there carried away
to a small room made out of cushions and
tender cotton candy for walls.

Her hands were slightly tied together
to prevent her from hurting herself.

During bedtime I swear I could hear her frightened screams.

On Sunday

On Sunday Mom baked cookies for me,
but I couldn't eat them because she cooked them outside of this "jail."

And everything outside of these four walls
is diluted.

And everything outside of these four walls
is evil.

Forever Loveless

So I'm sitting here,
remembering the day you asked me out.

Trying to remember if I was already as insane and depressed
the moment our lips touched for the very first time.

Remembering, as everyone else makes their phone calls home.

You said I was too young to love;
I said I loved you once.

I knew happiness wouldn't last forever
But the bitter sting followed by it would hurt a lifetime.

The sting of knowing I never had you,
and to think you had me more than once.

You said you loved me.
You said your love for me faded away.

But, I know we will lie
right beside each other some other day, love.

We will remain
like two loveless lovers,
forever until the end.

Sitting in Another Group Talk

I have to sit here and listen to
Tina talk about her weight obsession.

As Molly whines that the voices
inside her head won't stop their chattering.

And Yvonne shares her wild
sex adventures with the guys.

I have to sit here and listen,
for I refuse to talk.

Yvonne

Yvonne is like a blossom tree,
who greets animals with open branches.
And extends a nest for them to come lay on her.

She said she felt so neglected.
She said she wanted more.

So she let them sit there with open arms.
Willing to do anything for a token of company.

She fairly reminds me of myself.

The Guys

The guys never took me seriously.
They would always approach me with sexual innuendos.

I never made it to their mother's house
but rather to the backseat of their car.

It was all emotionless,
rather made me sick.

I felt my body numb,
my hips shiver cold,
my breast tender.

For I had many lovers
out of lust,

but not one love
out of pure love.

Perhaps they felt as lonely as I did.
Perhaps their girl was hard to get.

The guys never took me seriously,
so I figured I wouldn't either.

My love took me halfway seriously.
But I loved him,
and
he loved me.

Ryan the Looney

Ryan, the pale-complexioned,
Freckle-faced loony,
would always spit his meds
right after Bertha walked away!

I'm not sure how he did it.
I'm not sure how he got away
without getting caught by a nurse
like Bertha.

He tried showing me once,
the way he hid his Prozac
under the back of his throat and how'd he hurt himself
right after; the feeling of guilt haunted him.

Anxiously, he would scratch his wrist so hard,
leaving him with permanent scars.

Of course I never learned his ways too good.

Of course I never really paid much attention
to the loony son of a bitch.

I wasn't part of him.
Or any of the helpless, emotional teens
sipping Prozac for lunch.

I wasn't part of any of the kids sitting in the room chatting
as they wore the same insane, green-colored gown as
I did.

The ones you tie to your back
and feel as cold as your bed sheets
feel in winter.

Bertha

When she walks in, I curl up in bed
gelid like a frozen Popsicle.

She reaches for my arm
and injects me with a shot
of serenity.

Then asks me, "Is everything okay?"

I wait for the ringing of my voice to
respond, but there's not a scarcely pitch,
and when I turn around to face her,
she's already vanished

  ...realizing her question was moronic.

Therapy

Doctor Pathetic
witnesses my misery
under his thick, awful
Hitler-mustache and laments about me.

"Such a beautiful girl," he says.

Then skims under my gown,
undressing me with his stare.
He focuses on my thighs.

I then glance at the clock
and get lost with its ticking,
counting the minutes for me to be dismissed.

The Other Side

They say grass is greener
on the other side.

I wonder if it truly is.

After therapy,
I decided to find out for myself.

Curiosity had me marveling
How could it possibly be on the other lane?

I imagined finding something charming,
like a buried treasure full of jewels

or the sight of normal people
feasting on the joy of life.

But to my surprise
I found the face of a gloomy,
tiny one laying in colorful pj's,
tucked under the same ugly
bed sheets as mine.

That's when I realized I had stepped into
 the children's department of mental illness.

I guess grass isn't so green on the other side after all.

Restlessness

As you awake
in this city
of your own,
breathing nicely in your home...

I'm in here waiting for you to tuck me in.

Daddy's Little Girl

When I was three
I was the girl that shined through your pupils.

You would push me on the swing,
watch me fall,
pick me up,
and hold me in your arms asleep.

I followed you everywhere you'd go.
With you I was safe.
With you I was merry.

For I was your little girl,
and you were my daddy,
the most precious man to me
aside from Grandpa.

Now, that I've fallen once more,
You're not here to pick me up anymore!

Dad

Dad hardly stops for a visit,
I think he's comedown by me.

When he walked in today
I didn't recall his steps.

A blurry image of a man
sat right beside me;
stiff, he sat like a
hard, wooden figurine,
with a face as tilted
as the many faces of patients
breathing under this same building.

Rag Doll

He then pulled out a tiny rag doll
from his suit.

"Mona!" I yelled.

It was the same rag doll Grandpa had
bought me for my fourth birthday.

It had two dusky buttons
nicely sewn for eyes
and shaggy, red hair,
just like mine.

As I held the small doll,
crumpled up in bed,

the fine smell of rosemary
filled the room.

Then after hearing nothing but
screams of silent melodies
coming from Dad's mouth,

he got up, kissed my hand goodbye,
and whispered, "I'm sorry, honey."

Then a tear burned down his cheek
just like acid.

So...

I gazed out at the moon tonight,
hoping you'd appear to me upon a wishing star.

Or perhaps you'd hit my bedroom roof with the power
of a meteor and take me wrapped back into your arms.

I waited for you,
for your touch,

for the sensation of your beard
tickling my cheeks,

for your aggressive kisses
yet soft whispers.

The stars slowly swept away;
I saw them disappear along with the moon.

And when the sun came out to play,
there I lay all alone.

with wide open arms,
waiting for your return.

But you never came;
your image went away,
with the moon, with the wishing stars,

with my tears,
tears of rain.

Staffs on Their Morning Break

We are not allowed to drink coffee,
although I wake up with the aroma of it
teasing my insides.

I can smell the coffee beans roasting,
pouring themselves into these huge mugs,

mugs from which Bertha and the rest of the staff
sip from on their morning break,

in a room full of laughter
where they pamper with joy,
endless conversations,
and that tall mug of coffee,

which I crave.

Cravings

Like a pregnant women,
I crave.

I crave your kiss,
I crave your touch,
I crave a cigarette,
to pure my lungs.

I crave for coffee, so
I crawl to the kitchen
and get a hold of that huge mug,

then lavish myself with caffeine,
indulge myself with its sour taste,

the taste of you.

Morbidly Thin

The air travels at its electric speed,
dragging my soul with it.

Morbidly thin, I stand,
left with no soul, no piece of mind
under my control,

but these set of cold, rusty bones.

Thanksgiving Day

Salty tears,
sour heart .

No singing grace,
no birthday hugs.

Thirty milligrams of Prozac,
two cold turkeys,
and one birthday wish:
to get out of here!

Judy's Visit

Through thick and thin
you've been by my side.

Even though you knew I had gone
bananas, nuts, whacko, lunatic, mad.

You sat still the entire 1,800
seconds of your visit, staring at my engrossed bug eyes
and large, open jaw.

"I'm sorry for my ill appearance," I whispered
as we hugged goodbye.

Today Amber
Tomorrow, Who Knows

Amber sketched a beautiful scene of fluttering
butterflies today during workshops.

She shot a beam of light within her smile,
consumed her three daily meals, and swallowed her
expected lozenges.

During bedtime she hummed a melody,
perhaps out of joy.

Today she was Amber;
tomorrow who knows.

TV

It was a cold Tuesday morning when
Ryan ran up to the teal couch,
in direction towards the remote control.

We all sit impatiently as he flips
through the channels of our decent-size TV,
until he finally makes his choice and stops the remote
on the *Fox 11 News.*

We all fuss about his selection—like who watches the news nowadays?

"Nothing but tragic stories," I say.

Caged Wings

Grandma owned a pair of wings
which she kept imprisoned on her porch.

Every Sunday we went by,
the creature would greet me
with its extended peck penetrating
through its golden cage.

As other birds flew by in the
outsized skies, he watched them.

One Sunday morning, I set it free!
Free from its solitary world.

Before I ended up here, Father purchased her a new bird,
which she later kept right inside that same golden cage.

Phone Call to Freedom

I awoke to the disturbing, yet familiar sound
of a crying hummingbird.

Its structure was built out of
a palette of colorful feathers
that quite amused me.

Suddenly the phone rang;
it's my grandmother.
I demand that she'd free the creature.

I yell out at the top of my lungs
to un-cage the bird

until my screams are so rowdy
that a nurse has to escort me back to my own birdcage.

Released

The following days I must of been doing decent,
because I got a call from daddy and when I
least expected it, my bags were packed.

Hooray!

Back on the Ride

I'm sitting in the front passenger seat
back on the ride home with Dad,

thinking there will be no more of Molly's
screams haunting me at midnight,

smiling about the fact that I don't have to wear the
horrible green gowns anymore,

when two blocks away from my house,
we find ourselves singing along with the radio
to The Cars and their "Just What I Needed" tune.

Daddy stops the car
until the melody is over, and
we both smile.

Then I realize that all I needed
was you by my side.

Mom's Welcoming

Mom bought me a bunny,
a furry, gray, adorable creature
that bundled under my arms
in search of warmth.

It must have thought I was
its mother.

Mom bought mc a bunny
to keep me company.
That way I wouldn't feel you leave
as you dropped me off the porch.

I never caged it of course.
I enjoyed watching it hop in the free,
until one day it hopped far away
in search of its own path...
as I now search for mine.

About the Author

After the break-up with her first boyfriend, an older local guitarist, teenager Claudia V. fell into the deep hole of depression. Often thoughts of feeling worthless and lonely crept into her mind.

While being professionally treated for her depression, Claudia felt the urge to write. That's when the character of Amber came along, a young girl who is tormented by her parents' divorce, develops an eating disorder, and of course foreshadows the life of losing a loved one.